Every
Mother
Can Let Go
of Stress

Every
Mother
Can Let Go
of Stress

Julie Barnhill

Revell

a division of Baker Publishing Group
Grand Rapids, Michigan

© 2008 by Julie Barnhill

Published by Revell
a division of Baker Publishing Group
P.O. Box 6287, Grand Rapids, MI 49516-6287
www.revellbooks.com

Printed in the United States of America

ISBN 978-0-8007-1907-4

Unless otherwise indicated, Scripture is taken from the HOLY BIBLE, NEW INTERNATIONAL VERSION®. NIV®. Copyright © 1973, 1978, 1984 by International Bible Society. Used by permission of Zondervan. All rights reserved.

Scripture marked NRSV is taken from the New Revised Standard Version of the Bible, copyright 1989, Division of Christian Education of the National Council of the Churches of Christ in the United States of America. Used by permission. All rights reserved.

Published in association with the literary agencies of Alive Communications, Inc., 7680 Goddard Street, Suite 200, Colorado Springs, Colorado 80920, and Fedd & Company, Inc., 9759 Concord Pass, Brentwood, Tennessee 37027.

As women, we hold within our grasp
the power to change the world.

One family at a time.

One mother heart at a time.

We **don't** have to run for political office.

We **don't** have to write books.

We **don't** have to tell a hundred thousand
people the details of our journey.

No,

we can make all the difference

simply

by telling the truth of our life.

To ourselves first . . . then to **one another**.

Do you find yourself feeling

tense,

anxious,

strained,

worried,

restless,

nervous,

overextended,

pressured,

troubled,

frazzled,

hassled,

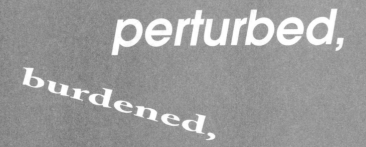

perturbed,

burdened,

nearing
the end
of your rope

■ and dealing with stress?

Just between you and me—

each word of experience, prayer, insight, gentle warning, and real-life proof of lasting change mentioned within these pages was first tested and lived out (for better or worse) in my own family relationships as a mother.

You are not alone. Thousands upon thousands of women have shared with me personally via conversation, email, phone calls, or handwritten letters that, yes, even tough mothers struggle with matters of stress, anger, fleeting humor reserves, and getting the blues.

The truth is, it isn't so much about getting everything right. Who among us reading these pages could honestly claim to have done that as a mother anyway? The important thing is acknowledging specific matters in our life as a mom for which we desperately need and desire change. And I can't think of anyone more willing and able to step up and do just that than me. So relax and stay a while as we take a closer look at stress and discover inspirational and practical tools to deal with it.

Difficulty that causes worry or emotional tension.

st re

Stress is when you wake up screaming and you realize you haven't fallen asleep yet.
—Unknown

ess

it is what it is . . .

A state of mental or emotional
strain or suspense.

Mom stress—
you've been there

When all you can think about

is the day they leave home.

Yelling at everyone most of the time.

Unable to set limits—for yourself or your children.

Reality is the leading cause of stress
for those in touch with it.

Jane Wagner

Okay, how many times have you heard or perhaps said the following: "Every mom is a working mom"? Well, guess what? It's truer than you ever thought. Consider your life as a mom as you read through the following top ten stressors *in the workplace,* as discovered in research surveys.*

---

*Accessed online at: http://www.hillsorient.com/articles/ 2005/08/202.html, October 29, 2007.

Stressor #10: "The Treadmill Syndrome"

▶ Having too much to do
▶ Doing the same thing with little outward progress to show for it

Okay, when's the last time you woke up in the morning—just laid in bed for an extra fifteen or forty-five minutes—and thought, *Gosh, what am I going to do with all the extra time I have today?*

Me neither.

My "morning" usually starts around 1:30 am, when I'm finally getting into bed after trying to get everything done from the previous day. I think of emails I need to return and permission slips for basketball practice, still on the kitchen table, that I need to fill out. There are at least twelve Post-it notes placed around my computer monitor—all reminding me of bank transactions I need to verify; schoolteachers I need to conference with regarding my son's academic sabbatical; football pads needing to be returned to coaches; college financial aid forms to be faxed; grocery items to replenish; and innumerable other details involving work, travel, home, family, and writing. Otherwise referred to as *life*.

Stressor #9: "Random Interruptions"

▶ Diaper blowouts: nearly always timed as you're leaving for a "must get there" event or appointment

▶ Cell phone calls and undecipherable text messages:

Voicemail: "Uh, Mom, I forgot my permission slip for the mandatory field trip that counts for 97.3 percent of my grade, which I've known about for twelve weeks but failed to tell you, and I need you to bring it to school now."

▶ Checking account overdrafts

▶ Emails from school administrators:

Subject: Your child

From: Your child's principal

Date: Today—*again.*

To: The problem child's mother

"Please contact the school office regarding the unacceptable behavior of your kindergartner today on the playground."

▶ A "+" sign on the at-home pregnancy test. *Smile!*

▶ Highly communicable pinkeye

▶ Toddlers wigging out in public

Stressor #8: "Pervasive Uncertainty"

Admit it. How many times a day have you found yourself questioning the choices you make as a mom? Or choices you didn't make? How often have you doubted your ability to do what you're doing—in the midst of doing it? I talked about this big-time stressor and its ugly spread throughout our lives in a previous book, *Motherhood: The Guilt That Keeps on Giving.* Lack of confidence feeds uncertainty and all but ensures continued off-the-chart stress.

Stressor #7: "Mistrust, Unfairness, and Family Politics"

If you've ever dealt with two children (of any age) for a period of twenty-four hours or more, you're sure to have heard various accusations tossed about:

"You like her more." (mistrust)

"But you let them (fill in the blank)!" (unfairness)

"Fine! I'll just ask Daddy (or Grandma or Grandpa) to get it for me." (family politics)

Sometimes you feel more like a referee than a mother!

I know my eyes nearly rolled to the back of my head more than once when attempting to appease the "But that's not fair!" Barnhill spawnlings.

Stressor #6: "Unclear Policies and No Sense of Direction"

Do your toddlers and preschoolers know how they are expected to act at the grocery store? Do your teenagers know what the family rules are about missing curfew or understand what they are to do if they find themselves in an uncomfortable, possibly illegal, situation with others? Are you able to articulate—better, perhaps—have you *ever* articulated or written down for your own assurance and knowledge, the core dos, don'ts, and big-picture policies of your mothering? If not, set this book down long enough to do so. Your stress level doesn't have a chance of being alleviated until you establish and guide your kiddos in the direction they need to go.

Stressor #5: "Career and Job Ambiguity"

If you answered no to the questions posed in the preceding paragraph, you'll no doubt be familiar with stressor #5. Being in touch with reality dictates that we not only know why we're doing what we're doing as a mom, but also that we take the time to know what all this mothering is about in the grand scheme of life. I refer to it consistently in my writing and speaking as "knowing what matters in the light of eternity."

In the light of eternity, what is your role as a mother all about?

In the light of eternity, what matters? And what doesn't?

In the light of eternity, what are your chief aims? Asked another way: why are you doing what you're doing?

In the light of eternity, how will you measure your success or lack thereof regarding your role and aims?

Big thoughts, eh?

Stressors #4: "No Feedback" and #3: "No Appreciation"

I placed these two factors together because one feeds off the other in our job of mothering. Day after day and month after month, we wake up children, pick babies up out of cribs, change diapers, towel dry wiggly preschoolers, fix breakfast, pay lunch tabs, drop off kids for practice, cheer from the bleachers, double-check junior high math problems we barely understand, cook supper, spoon-feed the baby, facilitate *friendly* conversation during a meal, wash dirty clothes and fold clean ones, read a bedtime story, tuck in the kiddos, offer nighttime prayers, and say, "I love you," one final time before closing a bedroom door.

What do we get in return for all our time, effort, and devotion? Sometimes a hug, sometimes an extra smoochy kiss, but often nothing. And while we understand with our head that this is altogether normal (after all, how many times did you call your mother into your room just to tell her what a bang-up job she had done that day?), our heart longs for words of affirmation and praise.

We do these things because we're moms. We do these things because we love our children. We do these things, yet sometimes we wonder if anyone appreciates us or notices any of the work it requires to do everything as well as we do. Admit it, you wouldn't be opposed to a ticker tape parade with children and spouse lined up cheering and waving placards pronouncing you "World's Greatest Mom!"

Stressor #2: "Lack of Communication"

We love our babies.

We love our children.

But having conversations with them is limited at best. And let's face it, sometimes we wonder if we'll ever have time for another intelligent conversation with someone who doesn't depend on us to wipe his mouth, fix her "owies," or tie his shoes.

Then there's the fact that, even when we do have time to talk with our spouse, a friend, a family member, or some other adult, it's all too easy for our conversations to be so kid-centered that we don't feel as if we've really connected with others at all. And after a while, that lack of connection can really do a number on us in the stress department.

Stressor #1: "Lack of Control"

Think back to the "Random Interruptions" I listed a few pages back. Try as you might, you simply cannot control much of anything when it comes to life. You can dot every mothering *i* and cross every mothering *t*, but things are going to happen outside of your determined control.

Babies will come into contact with germs and viruses—despite your taking abundant care to protect them.

Toddlers will charge full steam ahead and fall headlong—despite your telling them, "Slow down or you'll get hurt!"

Some teenagers will choose to learn the hard way—despite your thoughtful, well-intentioned, and protective instructions to do otherwise.

And Super Mothers will battle the urge to fix it all and control it all throughout it all.

Call me crazy but methinks most, if not all, of those stressors can *easily* be applied to the work-related mom-stress many of us face. The adage is true: every mom is a working mom, and now we have the stress list to prove it!

Question is, what do we do about it? Read on, my friends, and we'll figure it out together.

There cannot be a stressful crisis next week.
My schedule is already full.

Henry Kissinger

Stress is not what happens to us. It's our response *to* what happens. And *response* is
something we can choose.

Maureen Killoran

Soul-utions for Stressed-Out Moms

Our lives are made up of thousands of moments, lived one at a time. Taking a few minutes every day in which to relax, reflect, and rejuvenate is a great way to remind us that we can choose peace at any time of day. Choose peace and less stress by implementing one of the many suggestions that follow. Keep this book close by as you daily choose to relax, reflect, and rejuvenate your heart, spirit, mind, and body.

Listen to Relaxing Music

Listen to calm, soothing music at home or on the way to work, while working, and while going to sleep. Music has a way of calming and soothing the mind and body. Add some Chopin, Mozart,
    light jazz,
        praise and worship,
            or mellow R&B.

Scrub Your Skin

Yes, I'm serious—you need to scrub! Purchase a loofah and body scrub of your choice and literally scrub your body from head to toe. Wahoo! Talk about invigorating. It makes your skin positively glow as you remove dead skin cells and reveal softer, more supple skin. If you're the mother of younger children (six years old or less), you must do your best to do this first thing in the morning. It's an excellent way to get your day off to a refreshing start.

Hugs and Kisses

Right now, find your child or call one of them into the room and give her a long, slow hug and plant a big kiss on her forehead. Ahh, there's nothing like it for you and your child. Don't let the hours of your day drain away without the willful and intentional choice to touch your children with love—and a big, embarrassing bear hug and kiss.

Get a Massage

Okay, truth in advertising: I don't get a massage very often. I'm just not that into it. But I've had too many friends and acquaintances, as well as complete strangers (everyone seems to have an opinion on this subject), tell me how much it helps them as a viable stress reliever. So try it and see what you think. If you find yourself in the "touch-me-not" camp like me, simply move ahead with the following soul-ution and offer the remaining table time to someone who enjoys a massage.

Sweet Indulgences

Bake some homemade cookies—with your children—and eat them fresh out of the oven with a cold glass of milk.

Julie's Chocolate Chip Stress-Relief Cookie Recipe

2¼ cups all-purpose flour

1 tsp. baking soda

1 tsp. salt

1 cup (1 stick) Crisco butter-flavored shortening

¾ cup granulated sugar

¾ cup brown sugar

1 tsp. vanilla extract

2 large eggs

1–12 oz. pkg. of your favorite chocolate chip morsels
(I prefer Nestle Toll House and Ghirardelli)

Preheat oven to 375° F.

Combine flour, baking soda, and salt in a small bowl and set aside. Beat Crisco, granulated sugar, brown sugar, and vanilla extract in large mixer bowl until creamy. Add eggs, one at a time, and beat until well blended. Gradually beat in flour mixture until mixed. Stir in chocolate chips. Drop by rounded tablespoons onto ungreased baking sheets.

Bake 9 to 11 minutes or until golden brown. Cool on baking sheets 2 minutes; remove to wire racks or wax paper to cool completely.

Makes about 5 dozen cookies (depending on cookie dough consumed pre-baking).

Hang Out with Stress-Free Friends (if you don't have any, find some!)

Bad Company isn't just a classic rock band, my friend! The Bible says, "Bad company ruins good morals" (1 Cor. 15:33 NRSV), and I believe it's also true that choosing to spend time with hyperstressed people will increase your stress factors. So the more time and energy you put into building friendships with women intent on living with a lower stress level, the better off you'll be.

Meditate on Truth

Let me be very clear in this soulful instruction: spend time reading, resting, and ruminating on the timeless truths presented in the Word of God—the Bible. No other book ever written can speak into your life like the Bible, for its author is God Himself, the

Creator of your life and the One who knows every-thing about you.

No other book has God's supernatural authority to change your life, to speak pointedly and accurately to your individual needs and questions, and to grant rest and peace in the midst of an all-too-often stress-filled life.

So reach for words of life and restoration as you relinquish more and more of what worries you and keeps your heart and mind on edge. The following are some of my favorite passages, ones I've consulted throughout the years.

> My Presence will go with you, and I will give you rest (Exod. 33:14).
>
> It is the LORD who goes before you. He will be with you; he will not fail you or forsake you. Do not fear or be dismayed (Deut. 31:8 NRSV).

The eternal God is your refuge, and underneath are the everlasting arms (Deut. 33:27).

The Lord is a refuge for the oppressed, a stronghold in times of trouble (Ps. 9:9).

I have set the Lord always before me. Because he is at my right hand, I will not be shaken (Ps. 16:8).

The Lord is my light and my salvation; whom shall I fear? The Lord is the stronghold of my life; of whom shall I be afraid? . . . Though an army encamp against me, my heart shall not fear; though war rise up against me, yet I will be confident (Ps. 27:1, 3 NRSV).

You are my hiding place; you will protect me from trouble and surround me with songs of deliverance (Ps. 32:7).

I sought the Lord, and he answered me; he delivered me from all my fears (Ps. 34:4).

Those who seek the Lord lack no good thing (Ps. 34:10b).

When the righteous cry for help, the LORD hears, and rescues them from all their troubles (Ps. 34:17 NRSV).

Trust in the LORD, and do good; so you will live in the land, and enjoy security. Take delight in the LORD, and he will give you the desires of your heart. Commit your way to the LORD; trust in him, and he will act. . . . Be still before the LORD, and wait patiently for him (Ps. 37:3–5, 7 NRSV).

Why are you cast down, O my soul, and why are you disquieted within me? Hope in God; for I shall again praise him, my help and my God. . . . By day the LORD commands his steadfast love, and at night his song is with me, a prayer to the God of my life (Ps. 42:5, 8 NRSV).

God is our refuge and strength, an ever-present help in trouble. Therefore we will not fear, though the earth give way and the mountains fall into the heart of the sea, though its waters roar and foam and the mountains quake with their surging (Ps. 46:1–3).

Hear my cry, O God; listen to my prayer. From the ends of the earth I call to you, I call as my heart grows faint; lead me to the rock that is higher than I. For you have been my refuge, a strong tower against the foe. I long to dwell in your tent forever and take refuge in the shelter of your wings (Ps. 61:1–4).

My soul finds rest in God alone; my salvation comes from him. He alone is my rock and my salvation; he is my fortress, I will never be shaken (Ps. 62:1–2).

You who live in the shelter of the Most High, who abide in the shadow of the Almighty, will say to the LORD, "My refuge and my fortress; my God, in whom I trust" (Ps. 91:1–2 NRSV).

Those who love me, I will deliver; I will protect those who know my name. When they call to me, I will answer them; I will be with them in trouble, I will rescue them and honor them. With long life I will satisfy them, and show them my salvation (Ps. 91:14–16 NRSV).

Praise the LORD, O my soul, and forget not all his benefits—who forgives all your sins and heals all your diseases, who redeems your life from the pit and crowns you with love and compassion, who satisfies

your desires with good things so that your youth is
renewed like the eagle's (Ps. 103:2–5).

Praise the LORD! Happy are those who fear the LORD. . . .
They are not afraid of evil tidings; their hearts are
firm, secure in the LORD. Their hearts are steady, they
will not be afraid (Ps. 112:1, 7–8 NRSV).

Unless the LORD builds the house, those who build it
labor in vain. Unless the LORD guards the city, the
guard keeps watch in vain. It is in vain that you
rise up early and go late to rest, eating the bread of
anxious toil; for he gives sleep to his beloved (Ps.
127:1–2 NRSV).

When I called, you answered me; you made me bold
and stouthearted (Ps. 138:3).

Learn to Delegate

Who said you had to do it all? It's time for moms
everywhere to step up and learn to delegate. Granted,
a little training and instructing will be necessary—but
trust me, it'll be more than worth it as you hand off

responsibilities another adult or your children are perfectly capable of handling, especially if you can let go of control issues and allow them to do the job their way—rather than the way you think it should be done.

When and if you can afford it, consider hiring a housecleaner to help take care of dusting, sweeping, and deep cleaning—the rugs, baseboards, windows, and things like that. Doing this occasionally gives you a chance to catch up, instead of always feeling behind in your cleaning. Don't assume this will require a scandalous amount of money either! Years ago, as the mother of two children under the age of three looking to supplement family income, I put an ad in the local newspaper announcing, Top to Bottom Cleaning Service. My hourly rate was reasonable and my cleaning services were fantastic. You never know—there may be another mom just like me those many years ago in your town.

Teach your children how to clean the toilet, scoop the litter box, and put the trash in the proper receptacle—then let them.

Check your local papers or ask around in women's circles and find a local caterer. Splurge and order a meal for the family or perhaps a baked item everyone would appreciate. I've never done the full-blown dinner thing, but Paula Fergerson makes some killer desserts, and I have availed myself of her cooking talent many times.

Consider hiring a "virtual assistant," an independent contractor providing administrative, technical, or sometimes creative assistance to clients to help with overwhelming business and administrative-related tasks.

Perhaps you're a stressed mother working as a real estate agent, author, photographer, national speaker, financial advisor, personal and professional coach, or other professional, and could use such an assistant. If so, simply click your way over to http://www.ivaa.org/ and discover an excellent resource. Maybe a virtual assistant is just what you need!

Move Your Body

Start moving your body with regular stretching, which improves blood circulation and increases energy levels. Stretching is a great preventative measure to take as well—allowing the muscles, tendons, and joints to function better and work to protect you. And, hey! If the only thing you've stretched is your imagination the past few months and years, you may want to consider looking at a book (with pictures!), checking with your doctor, or looking online for proper form and such.

Exercise is a great way to relieve stress and manage your energy levels. It doesn't have to be a big deal. It could be bouncing on a mini trampoline while the kids watch TV or going for a hike or just deliberately parking farther away from your destination so you get the chance to squeeze in a walk.

Read, Read, Read

When I want to escape and wind down from all the stuff life throws at me, I head to Barnes & Noble with my debit card. There are few things more enjoyable or relaxing than snuggling up in a cozy chair or sofa with a soft chenille throw wrapped over my legs and savoring a new book.

Some of my favorite fiction authors include:

Jodi Picoult
Mary DeMuth
Elizabeth Berg
Brian Haig
Daniel Silva

Francine Rivers

Joel Rosenberg

My top nonfiction authors include:

- Dr. James MacDonald—James MacDonald has committed his whole life to proclaiming the truth of God's transforming power. As a pastor, author, radio Bible teacher, speaker, friend, and family man, James ignites a bold passion for God in every avenue of influence.
- Brennan Manning—in the foreword of Brennan's book *The Ragamuffin Gospel*, he says its message is for those "whose cheese is falling off their cracker." That's why I love and recommend his writing. It isn't about getting your stuff together for God but discovering how God loves and delights in you in the midst of it. All of Brennan's books affirm such divine truth.

Breathe

Purposely slow down your breaths.

Inhale for five counts. Hold for five counts. And then exhale for five counts.

Do this especially when you find yourself spiraling into stressful worry and tension. Busy moms will be pleasantly surprised at how this simple technique can result in a more relaxed body and mind.

Call a Friend

Call a friend, one of your "stress-free" friends, mind you! The last thing you want or need is for someone to trump your stress with a long list of her concerns. Call the person who is most likely to make you laugh. Call the person who can help you see the sunny side of the moment—rather than proffer gloom and doom from the dark side.

Go for a Leisurely Drive

Is there a back road somewhere nearby where you can simply roll down the window, hang your left arm out, and feel the breeze on your face?

Is there a park somewhere nearby where you can take in the magnificent colors of fall on the changing leaves of maple trees, or perhaps the awe-inspiring sight of a majestic sequoia if you live in the California Northwest?

Perhaps you, like me, live somewhere a bit less dramatic when it comes to natural scenery. If so, try a simple drive in and around neighborhoods—noticing well-done landscaping or homes—with simply the sound of your radio accompanying you (it goes without saying that this drive should be taken sans children!).

Wherever that road may be—get there and relax.

Go Cavewoman

Turn off your cell phone.

Shut down your computer.

Leave your iPod on your dresser.

Forget the television.

Silence the radio with all its talk and bluster.

And know . . .

silence,

stillness,

and serenity in your life.

Sleep

I remember the advice other women gave me when my three children were infants: sleep when the baby sleeps. Well, my babies are now twenty, almost nineteen, and nearly fourteen, and this mom needs those extra moments of sleep just as much as she did way back in the day of bottles and diapers.

Four years ago I was diagnosed with sleep apnea—after months of excessive daytime sleepiness—which is falling asleep when you normally should not, such as while you are eating, talking, or driving. For the record, I never dozed off while eating or talking—but the driving, oh my. On more than one occasion I had no choice but to pull over due to my fear of falling utterly and completely asleep behind the wheel of the car.

Being sleep-deprived catches up with you and affects your entire state of mind as well as body, and I'm thankful for the medical means (CPAP machines) available to help moms like me actually sleep well at night and function safely.

It's Teatime

Did you ever set up and host a tea party as a little girl?

I remember using the miniature cups, saucers, plates, and teapot my mother and her twin sister had played with when they were little. The painted porcelain pieces seemed as priceless as the bone china in my mother's cabinet.

Methodically I would prepare:

Cutting up Little Debbie snack cakes into bite-sized pieces

Brewing "sun" tea (a cultural phenomenon in the 1970s)

Covering a flimsy card table with a Strawberry Short-cake bedsheet

And setting the table just so

Let's embrace our girlhood, ladies, and rediscover the joy of having tea.

Call a friend or two—just be sure they are of the non-hyperstressed variety—and ask them to bring their favorite flavor of tea. Then go out and buy a box of Little Debbie snack cakes (not to be confused with Hostess HoHos—BIG difference!)

Set your table (in other words, stack all the stuff previously covering it in an out-of-sight spot) and allow the comforting sips of tea to alleviate some stress.

Face Your Fears

Being afraid can be very stressful. Consider the following to help you identify and eliminate your fears.

1. What are you putting off out of fear?
2. What is it costing you—financially, emotionally, and physically—to postpone action?

3. If your worst fear happened now, what could you do to get things under control?

4. What do you have to gain by giving in to your fear?

5. What have you already lost by not facing it?

Pray

I believe in praying real.

Life is too raw and difficult to do it any other way.

I believe you should say what you feel (or don't, as the case may be sometimes), because God already knows it. Praying real just puts it out there—no addendums, no disclaimers, and no pretending to be or feel something you are not.

Lord,

I am the mother of stress!
If it can be agonized over, I have.
If it can be imagined and over-contemplated, I've thought it.
If it can be picked up and considered over and over and over
again, well, I'm your girl.
I don't want to be so anxious.
I don't want to worry and stew.
I don't want to believe it somehow all depends on me any
longer.
Show me any fears feeding my worry.
Teach me how to let go and trust others more—like my own
husband when it comes to raising our child!
And reassure me of Your presence and power.

Get a Pet

I know, I know, you're thinking, *Get a pet! Like that's going to help my stress levels!* I'd simply ask you to hear me out on this. About six weeks before I began writing this book, my family talked me into getting another cat. A *house* cat, to be more specific, for all other attempts (uh, I believe there were four) to have an outdoor/indoor cat met with a certain finality on the highway in front of our home.

So we picked up our kitty and brought him home, where we promptly discovered he was covered with fleas. Stress! When I had to rush him to the vet to be de-fleaed, more stress. I wasn't a happy camper, because there was no one to whom I could delegate the job, and I'm not, by nature, much of a cat lover anyway.

Nevertheless, the cat stayed. And you know what has happened over the course of a few weeks? I've actually come to like the furry little thing. He snuggles up against my equally furry house slippers as I write and will often nestle on my lap and purr with pure contentment.

He's relaxed.

I'm relaxed.

However, your best pet choice may be something a bit less furry and less susceptible to stress-inducing fleas. Think goldfish. Or perhaps a parakeet. Even a harmless garter snake if you dare! All three are pretty easy to manage yet technically fulfill the "pet" plea of our children.

Pets can help alleviate our stress because they offer unconditional love. Even on our worst days, somebody out there still loves us a lot. No matter what we do or say. Plus, they can't talk back! And studies have shown pets can lower blood pressure. Stroking a pet has a calming effect—it can lower your heart rate and blood pressure. Granted, this is a bit impossible to do with a garter snake or goldfish, so you may want to go with the warm and furry type creatures.

Give Yourself a Footbath and Pedicure

Okay, the same hang-up I have about body massages goes for people touching my feet as well, so I've invested in some nice foot-friendly products to help me get the same "stranger touching my feet" look sans stranger.

Dr. Scholl's Foot Spa with Bubbles and Massage
pumice stone and shaver for calluses
one serious barrel-spring toenail clipper (this baby will
    cut through an elephant hoof!)
dual-sided ingrown toenail file
FootSmart Soothing Foot Balm
various files
toenail buffer

numerous bottles of my favorite polish brand: OPI—
Malaga Wine

Every so often, when the notion strikes, I'll spend an entire evening soaking, pumicing, clipping, filing, balming, and polishing my digits to perfection. I encourage you to do the same!

Take a Five-Minute Vacation

For many moms, vacation is the least stress-free time of the year—what with whacko expectations from the kids and adult pressure to get one's money's worth out of the entire thing. Gads, I can recall a trip to the Missouri Ozarks that nearly did us all in!

So, rather than mentally planning out another tension-filled week (or two) with the kids, simply take a five-minute vacation right where you are. Close your eyes if you can and think about the place where you'd most like to vacation.

Imagine the surroundings and the sights and sounds.

Maybe it's a kid-free zone!

Make it *your* vacation—no rules or set itinerary to follow.

It's just you relaxing and letting go of another piece of stress.

God,
Help me hold tight to the things
that matter,
Let go of the things that don't,
And trust you with the details of everything
in between.

Make Time with Girlfriends a Priority
(your heart and health will thank you!)

I've always known I "feel" better after spending
time with my girlfriends; now I know that response
has been medically proven. Research studies at UCLA
found that time spent with women friends provides a
biological boost via the stress-busting hormone oxy-
tocin. When this hormone is released, it reduces heart
rate, blood pressure, and the stress hormone cortisone.
Women can and literally do feel the physiological
effects for quite some time afterward.

Schedule Time for Yourself

Blah, blah, blah, blah.

I know you've heard this before, but it bears repeat-
ing. Determine, no matter what, to schedule time for
yourself. The activity really doesn't matter as long as

busy moms take some time for themselves. One of my closest friends carves out running time for herself each week. Another loves to do scrapbooks and schedules a "Crop till We Drop" session with like-minded friends. And another simply enjoys sending the children to Grandma's and returning to the house to walk through her garden and sit on a porch swing and do nothing—absolutely nothing.

Eat Healthy (Ouch!)

It pains me to acknowledge the following, but nutritional truth must prevail: there are foods that promote calmness as well as foods that can contribute to increased stress levels due to unhealthy weight gain and/or bloating. Consuming too much sugar or caffeine can easily contribute to increased stress levels. Eating fresh fruits, vegetables, and protein can help a busy mom stay on track nutritionally and increase her potential for less stress.

Think Through What You Believe

Our thoughts and imaginations matter because they become the things we believe. And what we believe determines how we live and the actions (or in-actions) we take during the course of our lifetime.

Lighten Up!

Rediscover your sense of humor. Or unearth it for the first time, perhaps! Laughter is the best medicine and we need to self-medicate as often as we can. Relaxed moms aren't afraid to laugh at their own mistakes—their foibles—or over-the-top ridiculousness at certain given moments. Share jokes with friends and teach your children how to tell jokes. Laugh at, rather than scold, a toddler's silly antics, and watch funny movies with your kids. They need to hear their mom laugh—I mean really, truly laugh! You can read more about this in *Every Mother Deserves a Good Laugh*, another book in this series.

Walk on Sunshine

Nothing perks you up like a strong dose of sunshine. A regular twenty-minute walk outside every day will give you a multitude of benefits and awaken your soul to light. During the winter months when sunshine is in short supply in the Midwest, I visit a tanning salon just to feel the warmth and heat of faux-sunshine, and I've seriously considered purchasing a "light therapy product" to help get me through those gray, dark days of winter.

Know When It's Time to Quit

I've always had a hard time implementing this solution. Maybe it's my "all or nothing" temperament or type A work personality, but I have a hard time calling it "quits"—even for a few hours or an evening.

Take writing for instance.

I try to work during the hours my children are at school (8:00 am to 3:30 pm) and to shut down the computer once their father arrives home from work (5:15 pm). But more often than not, a writing deadline dictates otherwise or I fear I will somehow "lose the writing groove," so I sit and type far past the time I should have quit.

So one evening I simply announced to the kids and their dad, "I need you guys to help me quit working past five. When evening comes around, you have permission to remind me respectfully of the time. If the computer is running, ask me first if I need to save any documents and then shut it down. But always ask me first!"

Guess what happened?

Yep. My kids consistently reminded me of the time, and my husband told me how much he liked to come home and not find me parked in front of the monitor. It's still a battle at times, but honoring my family (and self) with downtime is crucial in my pursuit of less stress.

Handling Holiday Stress

It's pretty much a toss-up as to what's most stressing during the annual Turkey and Tinsel season.

Mounting credit card balances.

Expanding waistlines.

Packing and transporting babies, toddlers, and their accompanying four tons of paraphernalia over the freeway and through the tollbooth to Grandmother's house you go.

Or (*methinks this one wins hands down*) telling extended family that this year you've decided to celebrate the initial holiday hours of Christmas with your own nuclear family ... um, alone.

Gulp.

This can set off near nuclear meltdowns. Indeed, there's nothing quite like the first time you, dear Mom, step up and claim space for you and yours during the seasonal madhouse of family tradition, expectations, and sometimes not-so-subtle emotional manipulation.

Trust me, I know, for it wasn't that many years ago when it was only-child me nervously explaining to my parents why we would be driving to their house the day *after* Christmas.

I admit a bit of hemming and hawing on my part as I shared my reasons for doing so: Kristen, Ricky Neal, and Patrick would be able to crash out in their own beds around 12:40 am, wake up on their own schedule (4:00 am!), create a delightful mess of wrapping paper and boxes that wouldn't freak anyone out, and then enjoy a leisurely day of destroying their new toys (you know *exactly* what I'm talking about), while their parents passed out in the living room for about six hours.

A perfect morning, I tell you, just perfect.

Now, my parents weren't thrilled by the decision but they understood (pretty much) and I knew, for that year at that particular time in our lives, it was the best thing I could do for my family.

There is no ideal Christmas;

only the one Christmas you decide

to make as a reflection of your

values, desires, affections, traditions.

Bill McKibben

So what about you?

Do you find yourself at a place this year when you feel the need to set some new limits or stretch some unwritten but nevertheless hard-and-fast "but this is how we've always done things" holiday rules and regulations?

Do you find yourself needing to step up and be . . . *gulp again* . . . one tough mother?

If so, let me encourage you to do so with confidence and grace, and you can start by considering the following tried-and-true tips.

First, don't apologize for your decision. There often comes a time in our family schedules, lifestyles, and dynamics when we just know it's time for something different. I've often said to others and myself, "It is what it is." So too the holiday ebb and flow. It doesn't mean it'll always be this way—it simply is what it is *this* year.

Once again we find ourselves enmeshed in the Holiday Season, that very special time of year when we join with our loved ones in sharing centuries-old traditions such as trying to find a parking space at the mall.

We traditionally do this in my family by driving around the parking lot until we see a shopper emerge from the mall, then we follow her, in very much the same spirit as the Three Wise Men, who 2,000 years ago followed a star, week after week, until it led them to a parking space.*

Dave Barry

*Accessed online at http://www.quotegarden.com/christmas .html, March 19, 2008.

Second, allow *ample* time to communicate the holiday changes to family members. Don't even think about throwing this information out two days before any big holiday festivity. Give everyone time to adjust.

Third, be prepared for grandmas and grandpas (as well as aunts, uncles, and others) to be disappointed—even hurt. This is to be expected, so be ready to reassure them of your love as well as your plans post–home celebration. Let them know when they can expect to see their favorite little ones (and adults) pulling up in the driveway or arriving at the concourse.

Last (and this is so important), don't feel guilty or stressed about making this One Tough Mother call during the holidays. Remember, it doesn't mean you'll always do it this way—it is what it is for now. Relax in knowing other moms have gone before you (this one included) and have lived to tell the tale of stepping up and doing what is best for their family.

More Tips for Less Stress—Holiday or Not

▶ Shop on the weekdays, not the weekends. Instead of spending Saturday afternoon at the mall trying to find Aunt Tillie some dusting powder, take your kids to the park.

▶ Don't pack your calendar so full there's no room for unexpected events or free time. Leave a few days completely unscheduled.

▶ Remember to get a gift for yourself and put it under your tree. It'll make a wonderful surprise.

▶ You can't do it all, so don't try. Just volunteer for the activities you enjoy. No one is keeping track of the overachievers.

▶ Try not to be driven by unfulfilled expectations and perfectionism. Not every house has to look like those in *House Beautiful* magazine. The holidays will be enjoyable because your family will be together.

▶ Save diets for later! Enjoy the delicious foods and holiday desserts. January 1 will be here soon enough.

▶ Only buy gifts for those you really care about. Don't be suckered into the pressure and stress of picking up something for everyone on the face of the planet! Oh, okay, it just feels like you're expected to do that sometimes. Nevertheless, purchase gifts for those closest to you and allow a holiday card to do for the rest.

▶ Gifts are not only bought but found by giving of yourself. Perhaps there is a friend you haven't seen in a while; invite her over for tea and cookies.[*]

---

[*] Accessed online at http://www.homeschoolzone.com/m2m/news/stress.htm, October 22, 2007.

Nothing you do for children is ever wasted. They seem not to notice us, hovering, averting our eyes, and they seldom offer thanks, but what we do for them is never wasted.

Garrison Keillor

Relaxing with Your Children

Believe it or not, you can relieve stress while spending time with your children. The following are some great stress relievers* you can generally practice while caring for children:

Painting/drawing. Next time you feel stressed out, grab some water-soluble paint or markers and crayons and create a beautiful picture with your children. You can work through your feelings in an abstract way as you and your children create something wonderful in the process.

Walking. You can enjoy the benefits of exercise and let your children enjoy the scenery (or exercise along with you) by walking with them. You can put them in a stroller if they're very small, or let them ride a bike or scooter next to you if they're bigger. (Or, for a less brisk, more meandering walk, let them just walk with you.) This gets you both outside, enjoying

---

*Accessed and adapted from the website: http://stress.about.com/od/parentsunderstress/a/stress_kids.htm, October 22, 2007.

nature (or the view of some nice buildings), and away from most frustrations and responsibilities. (If your little ones don't want to sit quietly in a stroller and enjoy the scenery, you can bring a cup of Cheerios or another small snack to occupy them.)

Blowing bubbles. This can keep your little ones happy, giving you a break, and can take your mind off what's stressing you if you let it. There's something calming about watching the bubbles drift up, and there's real joy in watching the wonder in the eyes of small children enjoying the sight of bubbles, or the playfulness of slightly older children racing to pop them.

Gardening. You can relieve a lot of stress through gardening, and it can be a great activity for your children as well. Even small children can help you tend a garden if they're able to lift a small watering can. And they will have a great time digging in the dirt. Watching seeds grow into plants can be fun and educational for young kids, and older children can take pride in making their home more beautiful by tending to the yard.

Making Family Vacations
Enjoyable—*Mostly*

Is there a better recipe for toxic levels of mothering stress than the pressure cooker of a family vacation?

I think not.

Cramped minivans and/or cars conspire against us (we didn't get an oversize Yukon until way past the time we needed it). And oversold flights and agonizing layovers at hole-in-the-wall airports can put us over the edge.

The actual vacation rarely meets, let alone exceeds, our children's expectations, and Mom and Dad are often left holding a frustrating bag of complaints, whining, and general lack of thanks. Trust me, I know what I'm talking about here.

There was that little trip to those Missouri Ozarks mentioned a few pages ago. We rented a lakefront three-bedroom condominium and talked up the thrills of limitless putt-putt golf and go-carting. The two older children remembered a fun weekend when we stopped there several years previously and were looking forward to going.

And then it rained.

And rained.

And rained.

And then they complained.

And complained.

And complained.

It was, without a doubt, one of the most miserable times I've ever spent with my family.

More aptly stated: one of the most miserable times I've ever spent with my oldest child. She was in a mood the entire week, and when a fourteen-year-old decides she's "in a mood," well, it's all over except for the incessant complaining.

Sigh.

I vowed never to go on a family vacation again. But I got stressed out thinking my children would never be able to recall fun, wonderful memories of time spent together, so we did it again. And it was probably the best ever!

So don't give up, Mom, when it comes to finding your family's stress-free vacation groove. Keep trying—pay attention to what works and what totally and utterly fails, and adjust your choices accordingly.

In the meantime, here are some great tips for making your time together go more smoothly.

Be Realistic and Consider the Ages of Your Children

Kids can tolerate only so much, and while I'm sure you would have found the Museum of Old and Boring Things utterly fascinating, well, your four-year-old child may not.

The best analogy I can give is walking into a Bass Pro Shop with my husband a couple of years ago. His eyes glazed over and a dopey "I'm in heaven" smile settled on his face, while I, on the other hand, felt as if I had entered the Twilight Zone.

I looked at Rick and asked, "This is the way you feel when I make you go into Nordstrom's department store, isn't it?"

He nodded yes and shuffled down the aisle, mumbling incoherently about fishing lures or something.

Ship Items Ahead to Your Destination

Man! I wish I had done this years ago when half the space in our minivan was taken up with baby formula and diapers. It's really not as expensive as it sounds. Plan ahead and box up durable goods (extra diapers, toys, shoes, and so on) in care of the hotel where you'll be staying. As long as you allow five to seven days for delivery, your cost via United States Postal Service should be well under twenty dollars.

Maintain Routines

You can keep a routine by continuing to do the simple things. Bring favorite toys and books. Maintain the same bedtime schedule. If your child always naps at noon, it isn't fair to expect him to behave in a boring museum at that time. Go back to the hotel for lunch and a nap, and return to your day's activities later.

This is essential for children who work best with routine! My middle child, Ricky Neal, could be your sweetest dream or worst nightmare—depending on if and when he got his nap. My oldest, Kristen, always wanted to know what's what with our basic itinerary. And Patrick, well, Patrick is my favorite child when it comes to vacations because he pretty much goes with whatever is happening at the time. Of course he insists on getting something to eat about every forty-five minutes, but I'm working on that.

A **vacation** is like love—anticipated with pleasure, experienced with discomfort, and remembered with nostalgia.

Author unknown

Perhaps the cover of this book caught your eye on a Store-Mart shelf, grocery store kiosk, or library display. Maybe a mothers' group or book club you participate in chose it as their monthly pick, or you found it lying beneath a pile of stacked reference materials in your physician's waiting room. Perhaps someone purchased it *for* you and/or recommended it *to* you, and, given the title, you're just not quite sure what to think. Or perhaps you simply picked it up because it aptly describes where you have been or the place you currently find yourself as a mom.

No matter the path that brought you, I'm so glad you're here.

I tried my best to set out a quick-to-read layout, easy to digest and easy to go to as a reference in time(s) of need. I included all sorts of quotable quotes that you can tuck away in your memory and use as encouragement for yourself and others, as well as truth found in the Bible.

You see, this one thing I know to be true: change—true and lasting change for our weakness, failings, weariness, and worries—can and will ultimately come as the result of truth penetrating our heart.

I know from raw personal experience that it is impossible to change oneself by self-will alone—at least any lasting change. Oh, we can vow to "do better" and all that jazz, but eventually, well, eventually we find ourselves back to square one because we're altogether human and finite and limited.

But the truth of Scripture penetrating our heart brings about an entirely different result. When we hear and accept the truth of God's Word, it changes our heart—the core of who we are, how we feel, how we act, and what we believe—and when our heart changes, our thoughts change. And when our thoughts change, our actions change. And when our thoughts and our actions change, our words and feelings change. And it is then, my sweet friend, when you see lasting change in yourself and in your family.

So if you rushed through or ignored those important words that I quoted from other people or from the Bible, I want to encourage you to go back and reread their wisdom. You may even want to grab a few Post-its and mark two or three of your favorites.

Read through them and ask God to show you a particular verse by which you may find comfort, grace, teaching, and change. Copy it and post it near the places you frequent: kitchen, bathroom, baby's changing station, and minivan. Post it, read it aloud, believe it, and live for yourself the truth it contains.

I hope my own confessions of shared struggles and countless discoveries of hope and change along the way have helped you feel less alone. I am more convinced each year I live, write, and speak with women that hearing and reading the unvarnished truth of someone else's story is paramount in our belief that we are not the only ones battling and struggling.

And last, but not least, I hope the personalized prayers touched your mothering heart and spirit. I get to do a lot of amazing things and have traveled across the world—literally—but time and time again this consistency remains: I find praying for individuals, one-on-one, to be undoubtedly my favorite thing to do. As you pray, I'd like you to imagine me standing with you—in front of you with my left hand placed on your right shoulder and my right gently pressed against the back of your neck. Our heads are bowed—foreheads leaning toward one another—as we simply talk real with God about our needs and His ability to meet them.

That's all.

No fill-in-the-blanks.

No tests or teaching points to ponder.

It's just you and me touching base in the most meaningful and relaxed manner I know how. So enjoy, my friend, and know I'm cheering for you from across the miles, cheering and praying peace, joy, contentment, and confidence into your life as a woman and mom. I'll look forward to hearing from you personally as a result of our time together.

Until then!

Julie

Julie Barnhill
julie@juliebarnhill.com
onetoughmothertalk.blogspot.com

from Author
Julie Barnhill

EVERY
MOTHER
CAN
Beat the Blues

Julie Barnhill
AUTHOR OF *ONE TOUGH MOTHER*

EVERY
MOTHER
DESERVES
a Good Laugh

Julie Barnhill
AUTHOR OF *ONE TOUGH MOTHER*

EVERY
MOTHER
CAN
Let Go of Stress

Julie Barnhill
AUTHOR OF *ONE TOUGH MOTHER*

EVERY
MOTHER
CAN
Keep Her Cool

Julie Barnhill
AUTHOR OF *ONE TOUGH MOTHER*

Mothers of Preschoolers

Better together...

MOPS is here to come alongside you during this season of early mothering to give you the support and resources you need to be a great mom.

Get connected today!

Mothers of Preschoolers

2370 S. Trenton Way, Denver CO 80231
888.910.MOPS • www.MOPS.org/bettermoms